DATE DUE

Demco, Inc. 38-293

JAN 2 4 2006

OTHER PEOPLE

PHOENIX **POETS**

Other People

PETER CAMPION

THE UNIVERSITY OF CHICAGO PRESS
Chicago and London

PETER CAMPION is a Jones Lecturer in Poetry at Stanford University. A recipient of a Wallace Stegner Fellowship in poetry, Campion is also the author of a book on the art of Mitchell Johnson.

The University of Chicago Press, Chicago 60637
The University of Chicago Press, Ltd., London

14 13 12 11 10 09 08 07 06 05   1 2 3 4 5

ISBN: 0-226-09274-7 (cloth)
ISBN: 0-226-09275-5 (paper)

Library of Congress Cataloging-in-Publication Data

Campion, Peter, 1976–
       Other people : poems / Peter Campion.
           p.   cm.—Phoenix poets
       ISBN 0-226-09274-7 (cloth : alk. paper)
       ISBN 0-226-09275-5 (pbk. : alk. paper)
       1. Interpersonal relations—Poetry. I. Title.

PS3603. A486O86 2005
811'.6—dc22   2004019423

For Amy

Contents

III

Acknowledgments

I want to thank the editors of the following journals in which these poems, sometimes in different versions, first appeared:

AGNI: "From 'Les Amours'" (46), "Nephew" and "This Blue Vase" (58), "From a Childhood in Pioneer Valley" (Web edition)
Court Green: "Wildcat Canyon"
Literary Imagination: The Review of the Association of Literary Scholars and Critics, vol. 6, no. 2: "The Elephants" (© 2004). Used by permission of the Association of Literary Scholars and Critics.
PN Review: "The Red Eye," "Two Doubles," "Miranda Kittredge," "Vermont: The Ranch House," "Hummingbird"
Poetry: "SFO"
Slate (www.slate.com): "Other People," "Poem to Fire" (© 2004). Reprinted with permission. Slate is a trademark of Microsoft Corporation.
Southwest Review, vol. 88, no. 1: "The Population"
Tikkun: "Tamaracks"
TriQuarterly: "Or Wherever Your Final Destination May Be . . . ," "Skin," "Stone"
Two Lines: A Journal of Translation: "The Infraction" (© 2004)

"The Red Eye," "Two Doubles," "Nephew," "The Elephants," "Or Wherever Your Final Destination May Be . . . ," "Vermont: The Ranch House," and "This Blue Vase" were included in *The Zoo Anthology of Young American Poets* (© 2004), edited by David Yezzi.

*

I'm grateful for the support of a George Starbuck Lectureship at Boston University, as well as a Wallace Stegner Fellowship and Jones Lectureship at Stanford University.

Many thanks to everyone who read this book in manuscript form. I owe a special debt of gratitude to Tom Sleigh.

I

Poem to Fire

Fast transparency that explodes the fuel and air
in the cylinder and shuts the intake valves and thrusts
down on the piston so the crankshaft spins and spins

you cut through all material that blocks your way
so fast that driving now past rushes and billboards
this pull to her could be your own impersonal presence

cloaked in the day to day of the malls and condos
all those wired sensors keeping on guard for you
except you flicker even inside the wet wall

where papillary muscle makes that sweet pulsation
in whatever room she's moving through this moment
under the cotton and the cool smoothness tinted blue

The Population

One of the feelings which returns so often:
I mean the way that winter afternoons

call back those childhood sulks at the window.
That incessant need to sketch in the people

behind the lichened shingle of facing houses.
Now, when evening gathers, the walls conceal

no lion tamers lounging with the lions,
no divers plunging inside an aquarium.

Just a catch in the stomach like falling:
sweet emptiness . . . which others must also feel.

Even hours after, mothers and children
crossing the bright street by the supermarket

cut such vivid profiles. And they have a fierceness:
like ravenous hummingbirds who couldn't care

about the thorns they thrust through to devour
the little beads of honey in the flower.

Or like themselves . . . Lucent apartments shelve
into the hills, the whole volume of sky

falls on the spaces between, and passing strangers
move with the urgency that darkness

lends them: their skins much brighter against the expanse
of towers, suburbs, and fields they pull behind.

Two Doubles

They wear our bodies unsuspectingly.
  Make love, or fight, and they don't know
that their lives go on like programs on TV
  we've muted.
                    But their gestures show
how she wheels around, trying not to trouble
  him with the sight of her smudged tears.

Or how his apologies fall to babble.
  Or how some clownish splutter tears
both of them up with laughter.
                          Are they meant
  to be our bodies in projection?

The life we live wholly as instrument
  beneath our souls' plot-mad direction?

No. Like slippery creatures they evade
  any one view of who they are.

Last night, our dwelling in the talk we made.
  Your story shushing us both far
into the wash of us. The living room
  that much more our warm retreat.

Then suddenly a dull, beam-rattling "boom!"
  Running outside to the puddled street
and craning
                from the house to the alleyway
  I caught the dent on the circuit box.
The wires shooting blue sparks in a circling spray.
  Screeching
                toward neighboring blocks
the car that trailed smashed headlight glass behind.

  Mist for a second flashed through
                            clearer

and I saw (the memory's printed in my mind)
  how they grinned together in the mirror

4:17 a.m.

That tremor coursing
down his spine, that eyelid tremble
while he checks his gut . . . he thought
he'd slogged beyond such fogs of denial.
Though here in the glass are the outlines
he held against himself.
He feels as if he's fallen
out of the pool of soothing liquid chatter
into this cube of yellow cloth.
Fingers knead and tug.
Mouth even tries a knowing smile.
And no revelation comes.
Except he sees how his face has misted
from the panting: how he shivers to return
to the wholly imagined stream
of you and I and he and she.

The Elephants

after Leconte de Lisle

Zagging from far away, a mottled brown,
they rile the earth to the billowed sheet
they run inside. Trampling a pathway down
through dune formations with his massive feet

this one in front is the old chief. His hide
a mural that the years have learned to crack.
His head a boulder. Ropes of muscle guide
the arc and fall of his enormous back.

He never slows or speeds the forward thrust
his tribe keeps making, as they leave their mark
in pounded sand, these pilgrims caked in dust
all following their lumbering patriarch.

Fanned by their ears, trunks jutting past the teeth,
they run with their eyes closed. Their stomachs steam.
Under the vapor, sweating runnels seethe
where a thousand metallic insects gleam.

But nothing holds them back. The burning skins.
The thirst. Mouths blackened by the desert swelter.

They dream the fertile kingdom where all life begins.
The totem forest where they had their shelter.

They dream the river cresting the mountain ledge
where a hippo floats and roars and splashes.
There, blanched by the moon, at the steep edge,
they would descend to drink through splitting rushes.

Soon, with all their courageous, plodding heft
they cross the plain, become a mottled black,
scattering, till only the dunes are left.
The long horizon trails their crumbled track.

New Hampshire: Two Returning

This seems to be their spot. They return each night.
By moonlight, or street-lamps, they take long glances
up the hill, as if setting something right.

They like the older houses: all the lancet
windows and lattice work on private lanes
climbing the ridge.
                    A view downward through pines:
the stranded freight cars with their doors chained.
Below the tracks, a river. Shattered spine
of birch blurs under water.
                            Sometimes he sees
her eyes the way they were. Sometimes in the glow
of strangers' yellow curtains he can catch

a glimpse of how it was. He turns from the road.
And then their car careening through the trees.
Her irises blue, contracting like a cat's.

Those Painted Grins and Sneers

to Aaron Lisman

Rain that pelted the roof for days here cleared
this morning. Boston shone through a cold glaze.
My hands to the heat vents, I thought how weird
that we swam, only a month ago, those days
in the Berkshires when your firm then furtive look
as you sunned on the dock said playing Stephano
had sputtered out.
                              The sheer resolve it took.
The lines you had to know down to the marrow.
These were merely punishments preparing
you for future roles.
                              While you rehearsed
those nights, I crashed at your place.
                                                    All was glaring
impermanence. The drunk on the sidewalk cursed
"You white trash whore!" at somebody's window.
Inside the house, your clothes were strewn on the bed.
You only had this place for the length of the show.

Discomfort slipped to too familiar dread:
this sinking sense I have that behind
the simplest words for what we are and who

lurks an impulse to break the very bond
the speech attempts.

                I wasn't mad at you.

And I was only amused the other day
hearing you'd driven out to Chicago.
But this morning in a flash café
that dread returned, when a writer I know
told me about her time in Mexico.

Inside the prisons she went cell to cell
clad in a Red Cross uniform.

                Each night
she typed like a maniac in her hotel:
the bribes, the beatings, gangs. . . .

                To get it right
she played the ruse for weeks, until near dawn
one morning, someone slid hotel letterhead
beneath her door, with the scrawled words "get gone
you don't have time."

                She left her things and fled.
This didn't exist. This seemed a movie plot
she could almost laugh at.

                Then the car ride out.

Beneath a tarp in a trunk, the air so hot
she said it hurt to breathe. . . .

                Her haze of doubt
become a throbbing dread, inveigling her,
she hallucinated past that sweat-fogged space
the forced-perspective prison corridor
cell after cell, until each inmate's face

coalesced in a nullifying merge.
For weeks after, when she drove through L.A.
those cantilevered canyons seemed "one large
illusion," swiped across the light of day.

*

Before your stage-call, the afternoon
I left, we wandered the estate's lush ground
designers had fashioned as Roman ruin.

Chatting, though listening also to the sound
of the gathering audience, I said, "I'll call
or send . . ."
        I'd guess in your show-time count-down
you missed my pause.
        By the moss-mottled wall
we walked beside, four masks festooned the overgrown
spiraled wisteria vines.
        They startled me.
Those painted grins and sneers seemed meant to flout
both dissimulation's absurdity
and its insistent presence, branching out
of human nature.
        Maybe that's not true.
Maybe it was simply the garish paint
grabbing and slashing my touristic view.

But how fast I recalled that moment's faint
panic, this morning, when I saw the look
of blank beguilement crossing my friend's face
didn't come from shock at the risk she took:
it came when she guessed out loud that any trace

of her infraction had been scrubbed away.
You remember how in Prospero's cell,
as the speeches flare then smolder, Stephano
waits for his pardon. He'll no longer "dwell
in this bare island. . . ."

                    Everyone's free to go.

That's how I felt this afternoon, alone,
maundering gravel pathways to the river.

Yellow crowns of the sycamores have grown
thinner already there. High cattails shiver
and the brick and stucco fissure into light.

No, not illusion:
                  those forms the skyline etched
on the sky, blinking in then out of sight,
made the city seem part of a network stretched
beyond itself:
                street opening on street
on where, these days, you walk the lakeside blocks
to your rehearsals. I could feel the heat
of summer linger in those jagged shocks.

And in the warmth, then chill, that vast exchange
seemed to occur through time as well as space:
in the way that, curled inside you, past change
the "you"s that you were face the world you face.

Other People

In the dream where the dead return but never speak
they sauntered up the lawn: my mother's father
and Ned Gillette, who was shot in the robbery.

Maple branches twisting between the houses
scattered sun on their skin. And it didn't feel
like an afterlife: bathed in silver shade

and tennis shirts, they were just two other people
with those stippled faces mere will had not remembered.
Mussed bangs. The little lines on their lips.

With kindness, and no need of me, they stared
from the edge of an element so complete
that sunrise, when bird cries from the roof

shattered the airshaft, was catastrophe.
Then minutes afterwards, I was standing
pulling the chalky paste across my teeth.

Confessional Poem

I love to open the marbled cover
and find these moments ripped from the year.
In this one, purple maples hover

while my parents and I appear
beneath like dots: as if background
were the subject of the photograph

and skin one surface sun has found.
Our eyes contract and gleam as we laugh.
I nearly wince to see that laughter.

You know the plot. How father and mother
and child will turn in the decade after
to experts at wounding one another.

How their balm of distance
will salt the wounds. . . . Like my own voice
played back to me, this picture of us

mocks the assumption that there's a choice
you make to become who you are.
And the jolt of that is what I love:

the lawn, the house, the gleaming car
are simply there, while the trees above
are so streaked that they seem tensed

to the same, fearsome, invisible power
the three of us hold our ground against
as our faces flare from the paper.

Stephanie

This evening a policeman buzzed the door.
  His walkie-talkie spittled static.

We weren't the person he was looking for.
  But his doubt was automatic.

Barking a woman's name, he glared at me.
  When at last he was satisfied

our story checked out, he explained how she
  had called in mumbling "suicide."

My meek "wrong number" faltered down the hall:
  lost in the glaze from a game show

neighbors were laughing at. And that was all.
  That feeble green. Dim stairs below.

But up and pacing now from room to room
  as headlights angle in then pass,

as I open the blind, as buildings loom
  in tiers of light on this cold glass. . . .

I see. . . . It's a sprawl of anonymities.
  And not some mere projected screen.

More like a swarm of little creature eyes
   spiraling out through street-lamp sheen.

And staring across the block (where earlier
   that squad car bleeped and peeled away)

I chatter at the air. As if there were
   some healing spell for me to say.

Someone would know what name to listen for
   and hear the prayer she muttered in doubt

before I jerk closed my blind once more
   and watch this light shudder out.

Miranda Kittredge

Gabbling away, she always seemed half lost
in her decanters' sparkle when I entered.
Grandson of more and more suspicious friends
after her husband died I mowed her lawn.
And listened while she told his dashing tales
of celebrity:
               "Oh. He met Kennedy.
Who loved to show each visitor the marks
on the Oval Office floor from Eisenhower's
golfing spikes. And. . . ."
                    Raspy from decades
of Lucky Strikes, she'd pause to catch her breath
then turn toward her view.
                     It seemed as if she heard,
under hers, her husband's voice as living presence.
When she paused, in her silence, as she strained
to remember, it must somehow have felt
more true outside her on the darkening coast.

Salt-tinged wind swaying her willows. Bird-feeder
swinging as swarms of sparrows screeched around
the plastic, seed-stuffed stalk.
                  Two decades past.
Thin sleep this morning like a skein of voices.
And she appeared.
             No hoarse "young man . . . young man!"

Only her standing there in orange rayon
while her neighbor's houselights stuttered on
above the rock-churned surf. That unconstrained
splash, and that gravel-throated backwash
circled beneath her with such rich amplitude
and deepened presence: the entire coast's
long arcing bluffs gone blue then purple seemed
a liquid space, a secret element
that she would lead me through, though words
would never pass beyond its darkened margin.

II

Nephew

You swivel backwards, sniff your mother's skin.
Then your blue gaze returns and scours the page.
It's difficult, this needing to begin
in the middle. People live inside their age.

And you are lost now as you strain to learn
how letters are made by lines straightened or curled
into themselves. How when you read they turn
to speech, and speech to pictures of the world.

Maybe you know. You remember how we took
the Trailways. Banks and projects lifted faces
crusted with snow, you climbed our seat to look,
and Waltham and Chelmsford whooshed away to traces

jagged as names shrouded beneath your shrieks.
Now, the family room is a warm hold.
You smack the pages as your mother speaks.
Only the story goes on inside the cold

where a bear has clambered from his winter cave
to find a shopping mall. He blends with the flow.
Lands a job, an apartment, learns to shave.
You flinch, then laugh, at the words he doesn't know.

Wildcat Canyon

Falling on
Jeep Grand Cherokees
on garter snakes
beneath the agapanthus
sun keeps opening
into the manifold
keeps promising
whatever all those people
slamming up I-80
want to move inside

(like kids who want to live
in the TV and
think they can simply
rip the screen away)

America
          the helicopters
banking the canyon
the rainbows off irrigation rigs
moistened lips on the billboards

all of it rushes
so ferociously forward

merely splashing out
wine for friends
                while sunset
slices the sword palms
feels incredible

that this is life here
where the news
babbles from living rooms
and air has the sharpened
sweet smell of
lighter fluid and lilac

feels incredible
that these moments
are their own ends

Lansdowne Street: The Dancers

Heads swaying, slow-mo, while their faces streamed
with sweat from pumping jolts, they seemed both centered
on their bodies and off somewhere they dreamed:
looking down from that new height they entered.

Off and on for a year I bar-backed there.
And stood to the side while the dance revolved:
lurking for hours in the filtered glare
that zoomed on the halter-tops and then dissolved.

Depletion. Blankness. Glazed bewilderment.
Looking back, I wonder if before
it ended, that year of feeling frozen meant
to show to me I was a visitor

inside myself: if watching while the dancers
shimmied and flexed their taut and beaded skin
was some unconscious way of hunting answers
to my removed but tranced incomprehension.

And this look back, this also seems some urge
to hover just outside experience.
The dance, that constant overheated surge,
recedes in my memory to scattered glints.

The dancers fracture to mist. No disco ball
dizzies the room. But past the violet blur,
intent in their sarcastic free-for-all:
the fire warden and the manager.

One night, before we opened to the crowd
I heard the argument they failed to settle.
The manager, nylon-suited, nervous, loud:
"But what could burn? It's just concrete and metal."

Swizzling a drink, the warden patiently
chided back, as if getting him to learn
some challenging concept: "But don't you see?
The people burn. The god-damned people burn."

Tamaracks

You who see us in winds   like warriors or
dancers angling shoulders against each other
we're forced by long gone choices   like your fathers
hugely and helplessly   like nations' borders

From a Childhood in
Pioneer Valley

Each Friday night in the ice show
she got those families to know
she was the stunner on the bill.

But they were weird. You'd never hear
their chatter pick apart her skill.
It was a skill that touched on fear.

Was like the way everyone knew
the whistle at the reactor blew
each Thursday at 3:00. But if they heard

it any other time, the blast
meant a disaster had occurred.
They'd need to find their families fast.

In her over-the-top rock song
construction workers toiled headlong
through the night to build the highways.

Then, bit by mechanical bit,
it all fell to industrial maze.
But in the silver suit that fit

like a skin on her body's curves,
during her leaps and agile swerves
across the rink, she made the ice

the base for an action all her own.
Watching her lunging, circling slice
turn to the center for a lone

twirl, so fast she was just a ring
of swivelled silver, human spring
of molten silver, you could feel

she'd cut the story from the song.
No one would guess where the real
story had gone. Unless in the throng

heading out to the parking lot
you were a sniffling girl. You thought
about the show. In the silence

you turned to stare from the back seat.
White ranch house, slag heap, chain-link fence
then aspen spooled above the street.

They seemed a film between the sky
and your reflected, webbed eye.
With a nauseous urgency

you guessed this was the time to settle
your future. You thought "I want to be
the woman who turns to liquid metal."

Other People (II)

For years there was a redeeming presence.
This vision of a larger structure cupping
all the detail of all the lives. It felt
implicit: veiled behind the simple moments
hauling luggage across a concourse
or watching blocks beneath a window turn
to squares of yellow.
                Back inside my own
blue smudge, the presence promised to explain
my mother's rage
                (propelled by fear that others
must be shadowed behind her finding her
a little wanting: common).
                Promised to map
my father's distance
                (held with his belief
that the same systems you learn and plan and build
with the others mean to humiliate you).

*

Patience would pay. The pain would yield reward.
The presence had that moral obligation.

*

Today in Berkeley
                    everything shines clear.

A jet descends across our window pulling
shadows along the silver sheeted bay.

My parents are a bristling warmth that some weeks
ripples up from the cradled receiver.
Whatever presence looms behind my life

appears only through narrow apertures.
Is a sparkle crossing this lucid plain
where streets and planes and trees are just themselves.

Other people arrive. Lips shine and move
in speckled motes of sun. And words emerge:
more intensely alone and more free.

"Or Wherever Your Final Destination May Be . . ."

Part glamorous, part penitential, tunnel
  follows tunnel. Then halls through the concourse.
  The fuselage. It's like long tubes that funnel
out through the dark, this exhilarated force
  so constant, even now, in the muffled light
  by my bed, to lull myself, I plot a course
of my own imagined networks through the night.

  Though they keep leading to that hellish hotel
  two weeks ago. Some couple's screaming fight.
Then the low moans, more screaming.
                          Who could tell
  what room it came from? It came from the blaring stack
  of rooms. And listening to those voices swell
through the plaster, I thought I heard the halls in back
  of me give way:
               it seemed those people's souls
  themselves were swarming in a ragged pack
through a brambly, whacked-out maze of knolls
  and gullies.
          So tonight: of every place
  I can call back, how weird that this one consoles
my amped brain the best.
                When I turn to face
  the glass, it's just our view of Berkshire Street.
  The flood-lit baseball park.

There's not a trace
of any nightmare forest.

*

Except in this sweet
chill from the air conditioner, now I sense
what it is that assuaged me:
the more complete
calm, that came in a half dream, as my tense
body finally washed to sleep that night.

There was a meadow. And a chain-link fence
vanished to silver mesh above the height
we must have descended from. All around
those other faces quavered into sight.

Their shadows stretched across the littered ground.
Stretched as far as the glistering sign
of a city miles away.
The only sound
was the wind. Though pushing on
over the shine
off power stations and junkyards, you could see
those towers scale the long horizon line.

1985

On an afternoon
I have forgotten
on the grass on a hill
my mother sways my brother
through the April air
some stranger's stereo blares
Peter Gabriel

and the enormous
sprawl of life below us
has become so small
so wholly beautiful
it seems the richness
that was promised has
come true

The drumbeats are
leopards and emus
my mother's hair
a black slash through the sun

If only for this instant
swaying above the highways

we are so free
the whole screen of the present
strains to hold us

Pedal Tones

to Chris Bergson

I guess your hand has fully healed by now.
Though I imagine there's a scar, glistening
where your doctor cut and pulled the row
of stitches she'd sown in. Just listening
when you called to tell how, after 2:00,
as you searched that club you'd played to find your case,
a pane of broken glass propped out of view
sliced you, made my imagination race
with spliced-in images from film noir.
Quick scurry from the room. Wrapped bar rag soaked
dark red against the plush of the drummer's car.

You guffawed at my excited fright. You joked
that worrying on the phone I seemed to feel
more pain than you had. In the hospital
where you sat with Manhattan's all too real
emergencies, your cut was laughable.

But as she scrubbed your skin, the doctor said
she saw two tendons, there, exposed below
your wound. Sheathed shiny white, traversing red
layers of flesh you watched the doctor sew,

those tendons get your fingers round the frets
of your guitar. That one-eighth-inch of skin
beneath where the glass gouged you is what lets
you play tonight.
                    Forced humor waning in
your voice while telling this, our conversation
paused for a moment, letting silence speak:
the way your solos use slight hesitation,
time made to space each phrase, and show technique
is no sly cover-up, but what for years
you've worked, to find down in the tune your own
feel for the structure. Anyone who hears
you playing hears it like a pedal tone.

At home alone tonight (the stereo
muted where Monk and Bach switched track to track)
I've longed for that skill to feel below
mere quietude, to let my mind turn back
on what, slogging from 9:00 to 6:00 this week,
I've let slip through my mind. But all I've seen
inside is a paneled door slowly creak
open on glassed-in shelves. A TV screen
flickering on, a full-wall window blue
with evening blue.
                    Riding above New York,
cross town from the brownstone blocks where you
return through mineral morning light to work
on new arrangements, there's that old living room.
My mother's parents lived there years ago.
And that child I was, face turned toward intersecting
currents where up- and downtown traffic poured,
still flashes back, as this wall I feel protecting
my remove crumbles and opens outward.

(How mesmerizing memory can be,
strobing the spectral rooms it populates.
Then it turns false and cold and far from me
as the ballooning sentiment deflates.)

*

Leaving town last week I drove the hairpin bends
bordering north shore coves. At last I found
the opened gateway drawn on my new friend's
kind invitation. Private lanes there wound
past mansions out of murder mysteries.
But turning down his gravel drive, I saw
his place was a simple cottage that the trees
almost entirely hid from view.
                                          In the raw
wind by the sea-wall, we sat till dark came on.
The nearby lighthouse shot short, timed shocks
of white through the sky. All the others had gone
combing. Their voices echoed off the rocks.

My friend and I stayed talking all the while.
Till I turned, confused, watching moonlight set
glinting what I realized was kitchen tile.
He laughed to see I hadn't noticed yet.
The ground below us, rubble knee-high grass
grew out of, was his family's first floor.
Nine years ago, a storm all thought would pass
hundreds of miles from land pummeled shore
with waves so strong my friend's and scores of other
houses were smashed to timber, pulled to sea.

(In aerial photographs, floodwaters smother
entire downtowns.) And though his family
still owned the cottage where we'd sleep, my friend
seemed to enjoy hanging around those crude
rubble remains. Maybe choosing to spend
his time there, he could reach, past solitude,
some memory's base. . . . (Beneath the mere emotion
swift currents ghosting below each note you play.)

Later that evening, huddled by the ocean
as the cupped candles flickered all the way
up through the scrub brush, I sat staring still.
And saw ribbed whitecaps stretching endlessly
through my own half-conscious overspill.
They seemed both a threatening vastness cutting me
down to size while I gazed and a source
art only mimics: true force and inflection
in curving wave-lines that crash and then course
down glinting mica.
                        Trying to hold
balance, I think of practicing guitar
together years ago. The chords you told
me how to play fumbling bar to bar
beneath my hand, you kept me on the time
by nodding the changes, carving room inside
the form. And you nodded too to make me climb
through flubbed arpeggios, your casual guide
showing both fundamental skill and real
discovery: striking just one open string,
for instance, hearing how the tune would feel
continuing on that one tone left to ring.

III

Gossip

She drove to our apartment for drinks most nights.
This was Vermont. Our view was just a sliver
of other houses blinking from the heights.
The only sound nearby was the flowing river.

But once I tricked her into guessing who
was snorting coke, and "what about those days
when the three of them . . . ," it seemed as if the view
grew windows. It felt as if my absent gaze

(while she divulged, then freely speculated)
instead of finding the shadowy hillside
found rooms our friends were moving through conflated
with the hillside. Everyone got naked inside

these rooms with each other, then put on clothes
again, undressed once more: both women and men
disappeared, and then appeared in who knows
what grouping. That was how I saw it then.

Later that same year she moved away,
the MFA in Boston. We were with other
people we knew and half drunk she seemed to say
(rubbing her clavicles) "don't let them smother

me, they're smothering me." But when I grasped
her shoulder, she recoiled. Our eyes didn't meet.
Like a flustered matron, she even gasped.
I guess to prove me utterly indiscreet.

Recurring dream: . . . I'm naked. In the woods.
No one's here, so that merely means I shiver
when the wind blows. The strangeness can't hide
it's where we lived, though closer to the river.

Supported by splintered pilings, overgrown
by vines, a house appears in the dripping blur.
Her being there would mean I'm not alone.
I crouch on the brambled ground. I freeze and stare.

And then it's only drapery that looms
behind each rickety window, smeared with muck:
as if the river had flooded through those rooms
then rapidly drained back.

This Blue Vase

shows more than the morning clarities
of sun through leaves then through these windows.
Each thing is imbued by others. And staring
at the convex glass, I see the falls
in the one picture that held me enthralled
while you walked on through the gallery.

Even back then I must have felt
the photograph's stark black and white
trapping the glow off tons of water
in the entire minute of exposure
one hundred years before we were born
as weirdly relevant: how barns
and long gone houses' clapboard sides
above where shadowed cliff-face slid
vertiginously toward the falls
reflected all my naive bewilderment
seeing what I'd thought permanent
turn so starkly half unreal.

But this morning, watching sunlight steal
across this table's lacquered pine,
I still sense, through the smallest glints,
your presence still fusing all I see with you.
Blue irises from this vase's blue.

Vermont: The Ranch House

Uphill that day a coyote howled no end.
  On neighbors' properties where they were penned
the hunting dogs went crazy. We could hear
  their barks, then echoes. Whether it was fear
or animal bliss, it sounded like mimicry.
  The dogs copied the cousin they couldn't see.
We paused to listen, ignored it. Words we'd flung
  in anger minutes ago still hung
around the breezeway. Your relatives' house we stayed
  the weekend in, the remoteness, only made
the silence tenser: up against the house
  rage infected those blue and orange boughs.
It felt as if our feelings could be consoled
  only because they couldn't be controlled:
as if we couldn't speak till the landscape
  (gone for an instant strangely clear, each shape
outlined in blue, each leaf-edge wet and stark)
  finally lost all profile in the dark.

Or is that the way I want it in a poem?
  This urge to summon up your family home
must come from wanting to return to every scene
  where emotion floored me, so I can scrub them clean.

Later that evening, with the parlor lamp
  shut off, you allowed my fingers against your damp

cold cheek. And across the room each family photo,
    fluorescing through darkness, gave a glow
of animal warmth. Which seemed to break the chill.
    Seemed to flow from a power we didn't will.
And that silence no longer felt like a silence
    so much as our region of the hillside, dense
with sound. The dogs still scrabbled in their joy or fear.
    The open "hoo . . ." still echoed: thin and clear.

Hummingbird

Dim sycamores. A cinema parking lot.
I was sick. Had fainted. A metallic blue
had funneled round me like a tunnel shot
through space: no idea where I was or who.

Only my body, throbbing while the force
of will combated what held it motionless.
Then mind finally managed to coerce
neck muscles to lift against the huge duress.

And I was out of there and standing here
by Bella Luna. People ambled in
past sliding glass. Each thing shone clear,
each thing itself, and the cold traversed my skin.

*

First early morning waking in our place.
First light extended on a single spoke.
Night-blooming jasmine leaving its warm trace.
Only a fast, dendritic tremor broke

the peacefulness. You lay right there in the bed.
Sun burnished your skin with a yellow gloss.
Only you seemed in those moments of rapid dread
to be sealed in a space no words could cross.

Pulling me down, the memory of fainting
spiraled to mind, then zeroed farther back:
a Moorish entry court, a spotlit painting
showing a cormorant in slickened black.

I was five years old. Had learned to say
"Bon soir" to the maid who led us in to meet
with General Doriot. Would try and stay
in my "fauteuil" for the visit. Chestnut Street

was thick brick in the window while my mother
(she worked for him) translated all he said.
But then. . . . Was he describing his own brother
in France? . . . He leaned toward me with his speckled head.

He touched his hand to his mouth, as if to show
the words were in him, were physically coming through:
the way I gesture in speech to make you know
no room inside me is locked to you.

But he was showing me also how the man
put cyanide to his mouth. Him lying there
when German shepherds found the path he ran.
Steaming muzzles to almond-scented air.

And in this cinema that took the place
of the General's words, another shot remains.
A network of tubes traversing black space:
the web of the city's tunnels, like veins

through a body. In the guttering light
of a room where their courses have intersected
people trade information to aid their fight.
Each person wears a name the man protected.

*

Out walking under the lemon bottlebrush
and spruce trees on that first hot morning here,
the hillside pathways unbelievably lush,
I could still feel the pull of the dreamtime blur.

When I closed my eyes, a picture of your hair
brushing your cheek, lips moistened now to speak
(and tease me and swiftly deflect my stare)
disappeared, too quick, beneath a sunlit streak.

If there was a way to break past that ghost
terrain, it seemed then to lie in recalling
when had the isolation hurt the most.
And it circled back in the feeling of falling

in the parking lot that night five years ago.
In the memory, the intersecting play
of sodium vapor and shifting shadow
gave to a deeper, tapered passageway.

*

And I remembered. . . . How I didn't stay
in my armchair. How once the General told
of the death, there was a descending stairway.
Walls with crumbled lath and freckled mold.

I must not have been able to sit still.
So Ada from Adelboden, the maid
who'd shushed us in, led through the basement chill.
She spoke no English, but her quick charade

of beckoning hands signaled necessity.
I followed her past dusty trunks and mirrors.
When I dwell on that chambered space I see
a corridor spiraled with yellow smears.

The yellow seems to ripple with the need
to test my life against oblivion.
And then I'm simply seeing Ada lead
to an icebox. She smiles and reaches in

past packages of frozen food and holds
a hummingbird. Compact and crumpled blend
of teal and red, gone liquid in the folds
of Ada's palm, the feathers and hackles send

little sharpened rays to the window-well
above us both. And above the glass to the night
where each honeycombed apartment's shell
of dream and plaster hangs its speck of light.

Sometimes I feel I'm speaking to you after
rising through fathoms of ocean. Fresh air
in my acrid mouth. The sudden bursts of laughter
and spastic joy because I have you there.

Then the words only make us more apart.
But these moments unearthed from memory:
here is where all the calls and echoes start.
Here in this formalness in Ada and me.

Our bodies are dark cathedrals around the bird
wet in Ada's hand. Her eyebrows twitch
summing up my reaction. Weirdly assured
or still plain scared, I'm trying to sense which.

Skin

Your other guests all tanked, all trickled out
to traffic . . . now that mole and marble sheen
was the center of the whole apartment.

Your skin my fountain. Terraced avenues and
fenced-off reservoirs where the search lights
swivel and dribble back, the water, dirt paths

all ramified, all spinning around us.
Five years . . . and the night returned to faint
traces of trellised jasmine and cat scent.

This phantom still locked outside the peeling porch
clawing the cellophane and misted clover.

The Infraction

Alcaeus 298

The perpetrators
                    manglers of ancient rules
we need to coil our nooses around their necks
   or heft our stones and   ]
[   ]

If only the Achaeans had killed the man
who violated
                    all they held valuable
   (the god-defiler) then the warships
      would have encountered much gentler tail winds

But in the temple
                    clasping Athena's sculpted chin
her hands splayed round that
                              goddess whose power divides
   all spoils. . . . Cassandra huddled while the
      enemy battered then plunged though the cracked wall

                              ] Deiphobus too
they killed and
                    lamentation imbued the wall

and shouts of children also
                    mounted
        spread and suffused the Dardanian plain
And Ajax entered
                    drunk on his mania
(and close to death since
                    Pallas of all the gods

    hates human sacrilege the greatest)
        There in the temple he grabbed and held down

Cassandra's hands and melted inside of her
beneath the statues
                    hubris inveigled him
    That Locrian should have learned to fear the
        daughter of
                    He who determines our wars
but She . . . as horrid
                    rage like a gorgon's glared
beneath her eyebrows
                    crossed the high violet waves
    such anger staining the Aegean
        And she convened the impassive gale winds

                    *

Sacred

        Ajax   human

all night
first   crossed the high violet waves

not even twelve

                      is alive

   o son of Hyrrhas   when

                     ] warships

Stone

Impervious sphere that a glacier left for me to palm
you shimmer then shut yourself with such finality
you seem an emblem of the friend who "shut himself"

His ebullient dope on lover after lover
opened the room and held us there so many times
and he rose from his clinical blear so many times

thumb and pinky miming some buffoon on the phone
he made it easy to ignore his slow erasure
turning us to the people jabbering to stone

as the two hundred dollars a week of powder left
only his dresser drawer floating with photographs
the moon of his forehead flecked by psoriasis

The Red Eye

after Hesiod

Even when the porthole was black I tried to scan
   for roads beside the page. And when they ran
to a slender row (like pixels linking to a string)
   I shut the book and stared below the wing.

So many times before, the same apportioned blaze
   must have rippled through space to hold my gaze.
Only this time, a newness infused the spreading grid.

   And the sense that this pulsing circuit hid
everyone I knew, that this mineral sluice was home,
   sank in when I turned back and read the poem.

My eyes dropped to the place where "snakes came out to mate.
   Scales dimly flashed.
                   Whether in love or hate
or both all tangled in their writhing ritual
   fangs slashed at hairless flesh, then drank their fill.

In the pits and in the tunnels, run-off dribbled down
   on speckled leaves.

And there beneath each town
and beneath even the clustered towers, molten souls
    swivelled and sliced through the mazes of snake holes.

Eager to move inside whatever form they found,
    they rose toward being, up through the iced ground."

SFO

How concrete the world was

the eighteen wheelers hauling
skim milk or   striped gazelles

throwing their sheer blunt presence

into the morning air
only minutes before

you turned from me

lashes and cream cheeks
lost with the saris and business suits

all those faces pulled through the blue

like parachuters in reverse

Days later and again
                    how close it feels

this thud of blood that comes
speaking the words

From "Les Amours"

after Ronsard

With all the boxes cut and bundled now
and all the checks sent out, the mess we sweated
and shouted inside has opened on an actual home.

You cut a path through your day and I through mine.
Only we seem to move inside this burnish
swathing our separate selves. . . . Memory sputters.

Somewhere in a book hidden on these shelves
is a poem that keeps returning while my mind
circles and circles for you. The lines keep circling:

"Before the force of Love, which cleft the chest
of chaos and commanded Light, the ocean
only froth, the earth all broken up,

artless, formless, random, revolted in space.
All that composes me was once this way:
revolting in the prison cell of matter

before the force of Love created me.
Love arranged each infinitesimal
piece of me, attaching each in its proper place.

To make my mind, Love seared me with his flame.
And only when this was done, he brought me
into this world, through forests then cities:

instructing me in this dance, backwards, forwards,
between the who I'm not and who I am."

Poem before Sunrise

This image of a hole
planted behind my eyes.

Swivelled whirlpool that curves
right through me. Central bole

sawed from the tree of nerves.
This is the urge that lies

behind the throb of seeing.
This is the barest force

giving up to the wish
of whatever greater being:

little transparent fish
dragged on its one course

through forests of coral flowers
seeking the break of day.

Whatever way this power
pulls me: . . . ok . . . ok . . .